MAPLE TREE

David M. Schwartz is an award-winning author of children's books, on a wide variety of topics, loved by children around the world.
Dwight Kuhn's scientific expertise and artful eye work together with the camera to capture the awesome wonder of the natural world.

Please visit our web site at: www.garethstevens.com
For a free color catalog describing Gareth Stevens Publishing's list of high-quality books
and multimedia programs, call 1-800-542-2595 (USA) or 1-800-461-9120 (Canada).
Gareth Stevens Publishing's Fax: (414) 332-3567.

Library of Congress Cataloging-in-Publication Data

Schwartz, David M.
   Maple tree / by David M. Schwartz; photographs by Dwight Kuhn. — North American ed.
      p. cm. — (Life cycles: a springboards into science series)
   Includes bibliographical references and index.
   ISBN 0-8368-2978-6 (lib. bdg.)
   1. Maple—Life cycles—Juvenile literature. [1. Maple. 2. Trees.] I. Kuhn, Dwight, ill.
II. Title.
QK495.A17S38   2001
583'.78—dc21   2001031457

This North American edition first published in 2001 by
Gareth Stevens Publishing
A World Almanac Education Group Company
330 West Olive Street, Suite 100
Milwaukee, WI 53212 USA

First published in the United States in 1999 by Creative Teaching Press, Inc., P.O. Box 2723, Huntington Beach, CA 92647-0723.
Text © 1999 by David M. Schwartz; photographs © 1999 by Dwight Kuhn. Additional end matter © 2001 by Gareth Stevens, Inc.

Gareth Stevens editor: Mary Dykstra

Printed in the United States of America

1 2 3 4 5 6 7 8 9 05 04 03 02 01

MAPLE TREE

by David M. Schwartz
photographs by Dwight Kuhn

A SPRINGBOARDS INTO SCIENCE SERIES

Gareth Stevens Publishing
A WORLD ALMANAC EDUCATION GROUP COMPANY

In fall, the green leaves of maple trees turn red, yellow, and orange. These bright colors are in the leaves all summer, but green blocks them out. As the leaves die in fall, the green goes away, and the bright shades appear. Then the leaves drop to the ground.

Maple trees stand bare all winter. In early spring, clusters of bright red buds appear at the tips of their branches.

These buds will open into small red flowers. Look closely, and you will understand why this beautiful tree is called a red maple.

Maple trees have two types of flowers — male and female. Male flowers have many stalks, called stamens. Each stamen has a little knob called an anther on it. Anthers produce a fine yellow powder called pollen. Wind blows pollen from flower to flower, or insects move it as they visit flowers to feed on nectar.

When pollen lands on female flowers, it sticks to Y-shaped stalks called stigmas and fertilizes the female flower so that new seeds will form.

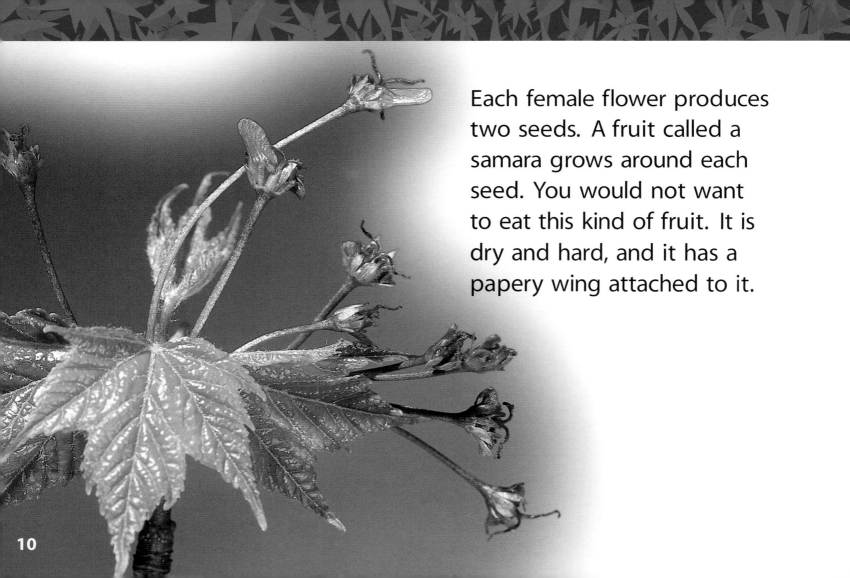

Each female flower produces two seeds. A fruit called a samara grows around each seed. You would not want to eat this kind of fruit. It is dry and hard, and it has a papery wing attached to it.

Samaras begin to grow when a tree gets its new spring leaves. By early summer, the samaras are hanging in ripe clusters. The wind shakes them from the tree, and their papery wings carry them spinning to the ground like little helicopters.

In moist soil, a maple seed can sprout in just a few days. A root grows in the soil, and a stem pushes upward through the soil, lifting the samara's wing into the air.

The wing soon falls off, and two leaves open. They are called seed leaves. Then other leaves open. The seed has now become a seedling.

New leaves grow from a bud at the very top of the plant. The leaves always come in pairs, one right across the stem from the other. Many more leaves appear as the seedling grows taller. The leaves make food for the whole plant.

It takes many years for a maple seedling to become a full-grown maple tree. As the seedling grows, its trunk gets taller and thicker. Branches grow from the trunk, twigs grow from the branches, and leaves grow on the twigs. In fall, when maple leaves drop to the ground, buds stay on the twigs.

The buds will form new flowers, seeds, and leaves in spring, and the life cycle of the maple tree will begin again.

Can you put these steps in the
life cycle of a maple tree in order?

Answer

GLOSSARY

anther: the knoblike part on a flower's stamen that produces and holds pollen.

buds: small, rounded swellings or growths on a stem or a branch, which contain leaves or flowers that are not fully developed.

clusters: things growing together in groups.

fertilizes: brings male and female cells together so a new plant or animal can grow.

moist: a little wet; damp.

nectar: the sweet liquid in flowers that many insects and birds like to drink.

pollen: the powdery yellow grains in flowers that contain male plant cells.

samara: the hard, dry fruit of some kinds of trees, including maples, which has a wing attached and usually contains only one seed.

seed leaves: the first pair of leaves that appear after a seed sprouts.

seedling: a very young plant that has sprouted from a seed.

shades: the many varieties of a single color, from light tones to dark tones.

stamens: the stalklike parts of male flowers to which anthers are attached.

stigmas: the Y-shaped stalks of female flowers, which receive pollen carried by wind or insects to fertilize a plant and start new growth.

ACTIVITIES

Leaf People

Collect leaves from different kinds of trees. Place them first between paper towels or pieces of newspaper, then put them between the pages of a large book. Carefully close the book and put something heavy on top of it. After a few days, the leaves will be dried out and flattened. Then you can make "leaf people" by arranging and gluing the leaves onto construction paper. What interesting characters can you make?

There's the Rub

Place a variety of leaves on several layers of newspaper. One leaf at a time, put a piece of clean paper on top of the leaf and rub over the paper with the side of a crayon. Press hard enough to show the leaf's outline and the pattern of its veins. Use your leaf rubbings for wrapping paper or to make greeting cards.

A Tree for All Seasons

Find a special tree near your home and make a scrapbook about it. Include photographs or drawings of how the tree looks at different times of the year. You can also include seeds you collect from around the tree, some pressed leaves, or a crayon rubbing of the tree's bark. Try to write the tree's "biography," from when it was a seedling to the present day.

Go on a Key Quest

The winged seeds, or samaras, that fall from maple trees are sometimes called keys. Go on a key quest at a park or a nature center. Look for samaras from different kinds of trees. Do any of the samaras match the pictures in this book? Collect samples of all the keys you find so you can sort and identify them at home.

More Books to Read

Berries, Nuts, and Seeds. Young Naturalist Field Guides (series). Diane L. Burns (Gareth Stevens)

From Acorn to Oak Tree. How Things Grow (series). Jan Kottke (Children's Press)

Look Once, Look Again: Plant Fruits & Seeds. David M. Schwartz (Gareth Stevens)

Maple Trees. Marcia S. Freeman (Pebble Books)

The Secret Life of Trees. Eyewitness Readers (series). Barbara Shook Hazen (DK Publishing)

Trees Are Terrific. Ranger Rick's Naturescope (series). National Wildlife Federation (McGraw-Hill)

Videos

Once There Was a Tree. (GPN)

Tell Me Why, Vol. 3: Flowers, Plants, and Trees. (Prism Entertainment)

Tree. (DK Vision)

Web Sites

www.domtar.com/arbre/english/start2.htm

www.inhs.uiuc.edu/chf/pub/tree_kit/student/

www.treetures.com/Blossom.htm

Some web sites stay current longer than others. For additional web sites, use a good search engine to locate the following topics: *maple trees, samaras, seeds,* and *trees.*

INDEX

anthers 8

branches 6, 16
buds 6, 7, 14, 16, 17

colors 5

fall 5, 16
fertilizing 9
flowers 7, 8, 9, 10, 17
food 14
fruit 10

insects 8

leaves 5, 11, 12, 14, 16, 17

nectar 8

pollen 8, 9

roots 12

samaras 10, 11, 12
seedlings 12, 14, 16
seeds 9, 10, 12, 17
soil 12
spring 6, 11, 17
sprouting 12
stamens 8
stems 12, 14
stigmas 9
summer 5, 11

trunks 16
twigs 16

wind 8, 11
winter 6